RATS,
FROGS AND BOGS OF London

First published in 2002 by Watling St Publishing
The Old Chapel
East End
Northleach
Gloucestershire
GL54 3PQ

Printed in Thailand

Copyright © Watling St Publishing Ltd 2002

All rights reserved. No part of this publication may be reproduced, stored in a retrieval system, or transmitted by any means, electronic, mechanical, photocopying, recording or otherwise, without the prior permission of the copyright holder.

ISBN 1-904153-05-4

24681097531

Cover design and illustration: Mark Davis
Cartoons: Martin Angel

Chris McLaren

WATLING STREET

Chris McLaren is a keen amateur naturalist. His day job is in publishing.

This book is for Calum and Leah

Contents

Introduction

What Will You Find Here?

It might be easier to say first of all what you won't find here. We don't have room to describe all the creatures you will find in London today - such a book would be even heavier than the latest Harry Potter. What we are are going to look at are some of the fantastic animals that are living right under our noses (and over our heads) in our capital city - and which just might surprise the careful watcher. Did you know that grass-snakes, parakeets and stag beetles have found a home here? Not to mention weasels, slow worms and great crested newts. Of course we don't want to ignore such lovable creatures as hedgehogs, woodpeckers, porpoises or fallow deer. (Yes, they're all here!) Nor should we avoid rooting around to discover the sewer rats (well, perhaps we could avoid rooting around for those!), signal crayfish, scorpions and an army of other crawling creatures that over the years have come to live in our city from far and wide.

This is not to ignore or dismiss the more familiar furry, feathery and scaly inhabitants of London. These all hold an important place in our lives. But we are about to go looking for the unusual, the wonderful, the amusing and the rather more creepy beings that are our close neighbours in this big city.

None of these creatures could exist, of course, if they didn't have anywhere suitable to live. For a city that's so full of people, cars and buildings, there is a surprising amount of green space in London - over 1500 square kilometres, in fact. And, more excitingly, around half of that is valuable to wildlife! Gardens, parks, meadows, railway embankments, heaths, marshes, ponds, lakes, reservoirs, canals, riverbanks, cemeteries and woodland all provide homes for the capital's animal kingdom. So if you keep your eyes peeled, know where to look, and are prepared to be patient, you could turn London into your own fantastic urban safari.

So let's begin our adventure trail around the leafy and watery green spaces of this huge, never-sleeping place. If you can get your hands on a good (and light) field guide, to help you identify what you're looking for, you're about to have a very rewarding time. You can either borrow or buy a book that covers one type of animal (for example, a bird guide) or a book that covers several. A notepad, a pair of binoculars and a magnifying glass will also come in very handy.

CHAPTER ONE

Talons, Beaks and Feathery Friends

London's Birds

If I were to tell you that the fastest animal in the world (possibly the fastest animal there has ever been) lives right in the heart of London, then you might think I've been at the bird seed again. But it does! And what's more, it's beginning to increase in numbers after having been made almost extinct in the south-east of England.

I'm talking about the Peregrine Falcon, which has been recorded swooping down on its prey at speeds of up to 220 miles per hour!

A Fatal Attraction – to Pigeons

Peregrines are very fond of a tasty pigeon, and strangely that was what nearly brought this magnificent hunter to an untimely end.

Before the Second World War began in 1939, gamekeepers would patrol the estates of grand houses, trapping and poisoning these incredible birds (which they thought of as troublesome pests) in order to save their precious game birds, such as pheasants and partridges. (Which, in fact, were only being saved for a nasty fate in the shooting season!).

During the war, many of these gamekeepers were called up to serve their country as soldiers, and of course these farms and estates were left largely unpatrolled. This meant that for a short while some relief was brought to the Peregrine Falcon, whiich was finding it very difficult to find a good square meal.

Sadly for some peregrines, this relief was to be short-lived because the British Armed Forces took to using racing pigeons as a means of delivering secret messages to and from France. And we know what the Peregrine Falcon's favourite dish was, don't we?

Most of southern England's peregrines, at that time, lived along the cliffs of the south coast. As soon as a racing pigeon went past a perching peregrine, carrying a secret message of grave national importance, guess what popped into the pergregrine's mind? Lunch! Naturally enough, this was more important to the peregrine than Britain's security, but the British Military saw things differently. They began to eradicate this bird all along the south coast.

You would think that when the war came to an end in 1945, the Peregrine's troubles would be over and it could once again feast on pigeons. But I'm afraid you'd be wrong. One thing that was made very clear to the government during the war was that we had to produce our own food in much larger quantities than ever before. Before the Second World War, we had imported a lot of food, but being an island - and being suddenly cut off from Europe after the war had started - made us very vulnerable.

And hungry.

And so great efforts were made to 'improve' the state of farming across the length and breadth of the land. These so-called improvements ultimately proved to be disastrous to the health of British wildlife and today the countryside is still suffering from this drive to produce more food. This was particularly true for the Peregrine Falcon, which sits at the top of its food chain.

Can you guess what one thing nearly finished off the beautiful Peregrine Falcon? Was it:

A) A blinding disease that attacks only peregrines

B) Too may aeroplanes in the air

C) Man

D) Not enough pigeons

Answer: C) We shouldn't be proud to admit that Man is the most dangerous animal that has ever lived. The Peregrine has suffered shooting, poisoning and other dastardly fates at our hands.

Where Do I Sit in the Food Chain?

We are at the very top of the human food chain (unless we are very silly or unlucky and get eaten by a lion or a tiger or a shark!). In other words, we eat the animals that eat the plants.

The food chain for a peregrine is much the same. It eats the pigeons that eat the grain.

In order to grow more crops farmers began to use more and more deadly poisons to kill the insects that attacked the young shoots. DDT (I won't give you its proper name as it's too difficult to spell!) was one of these poisons and a pretty deadly one at that. This is what happened:

Step 1 DDT was sprayed on the barley and other crops

Step 2 The pigeons ate the barley

Step 3 The peregrines ate the pigeons

Step 4 The poison that had passed through the chain had the effect of making the shell of the Peregrine's eggs very thin. So thin, in fact, that when the female Peregrine (who is rather bigger than the male) sat on her eggs, she broke them.

As a result, the population crashed and the bird looked as if it was doomed once again. Thankfully, DDT was eventually banned and the magnificent peregrine once again stood a chance of recovering.

The White Cliffs of London

We have learned that peregrines like to nest on cliffs and that they enjoy a pigeon or ten. Well, guess what London has plenty of - yes, pigeons and cliffs. Not real cliffs, of course, but tall buildings that look just like cliffs to your average peregrine falcon. They have gradually begun to make an appearance in London and are already breeding in a few spots. In fact, they look set to spread across much of the centre as they already have in other cities, such as New York.

The best place to see peregrine falcons in London is perhaps at Battersea Power Station, where they have nested, or at a variety of spots further down the river, including the South Bank Centre and Tate Modern, which used to be the Bankside Power Station. Have a look too in Trafalgar Square (lots of pigeons there) or in the vicinity of Charing Cross Hospital.

The most common raptor (raptor is just a posh word for bird of prey) in London is the **Kestrel**. This is the bird you see hovering over motorway verges or over scrubby grass in search of its favourite meals - bank voles and field mice. You could encounter them just about anywhere in the city where there is sufficient unkempt grassland and somewhere to nest, such as an old crow's nest or even the ledge of a building.

After the Kestrel, the next species of bird of prey you are likely to meet is the **Sparrowhawk**, which can often be seen pursuing small birds through the back gardens of many of the more wooded parts of London or dashing between the trees in many of the Central London parks. This species is currently increasing in the capital. One of the fascinating things about the Sparrowhawk is that, if it fails to capture its prey in flight, it will chase its poor victim on foot!

In the days of King Henry VIII, the Sparrowhawk, like the Peregrine, was bred and kept as a hunting bird. There was a strict rule as to who could 'fly' which kind of bird:

Emperor	**Golden Eagle**
King	**Gyrefalcon**
Prince	**Female Peregrine**
Knight	**Saker Falcon**
Squire	**Lanner Falcon**
Lady	**Merlin**
Page	**Hobby**
Poor Man	**Goshawk**
Priest	**Female Sparrowhawk**

It may surprise even your mad bird-watching uncle that the **Hobby** is, following the Sparrowhawk, next in line for London's most frequently spotted raptor. It even breeds here in small numbers. This fact is all the more amazing as there are less than one thousand pairs in the whole of Britain (although most of these are to be found in the south-eastern areas of the country, which is where London is situated, of course). The

Hobby is a summer visitor (unlike his cousins above), who arrives in April and departs in September. The Hobby likes to dine on dragonflies, swallows and martins and this is a good clue as to where you might find them. London is surrounded by reservoirs, marshes and large (and often disused) sewage farms. Such places are alive with swarming insects (including the Dragonfly), the favoured snack of swallows and martins.

Flying Kite

In the Middle Ages the sky was often black with circling, gliding flocks of **black kites**. When a body was spotted (and, yes, this may well often have been a human body) the kites would descend like vultures upon the carcass and tear into its flesh until only the bones were left. While black kites have long been lost from Britain their close relative, the **Red Kite**, has hung on, in small numbers, in the mountains of Wales. Recently, however, Scandinavian birds have been released by English Heritage at a site very near to the west of London, and these wonderful fork-tailed birds are increasingly spotted over the capital. It may not be long before a few pairs breed within the confines of the M25 orbital ring-road.

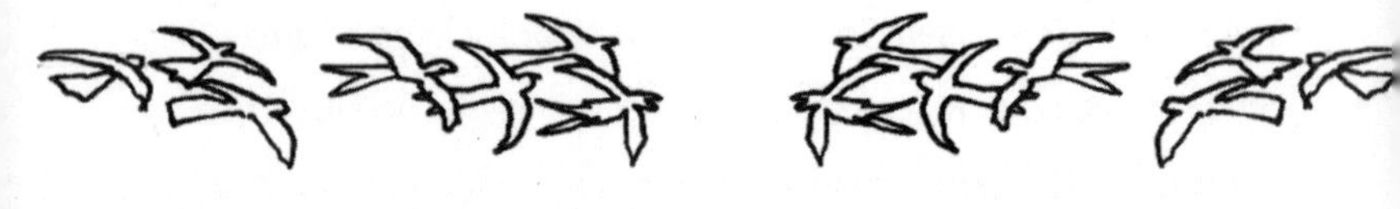

Before we move on from this fascinating genus (think of this as another word for group), there are one or two others which you might be lucky enough to spy. The **Common Buzzard** is gradually spreading east and birds occasionally turn up around the edges of London. **Ospreys** too pass through on migration (this is the journey some birds make to and from their summer and winter homes) to pick up a fish from the city's reservoirs.

Swanning Around

If there is one bird which takes pride of place in the history of London then the **Mute Swan** would be a major contender - if for no other reason than it is the biggest bird you will encounter in the entire British Isles. British mute swans are said to be the property of the Crown (the Queen). Having a swan for your dinner was once a sign of very high status in England, but thankfully that tradition has died out, and we made do with chicken - and turkey once a year!

The Mute Swan can be found on most reservoirs, rivers and ponds of any decent size in London. On the Thames Estuary you might also be lucky enough to find winter-visiting **bewick's** and **whooper swans**.

The **Ruddy Duck** has only recently made its home here in the United Kingdom, having been introduced from its real home in America. It is a most curious-looking bird with a stiff pointy tail and an unusual and beautiful pale blue bill. Although not many pairs breed here, reasonably good numbers settle in the area for winter. Possibly the best places to see a ruddy duck in London is at Hilfield Park Reservoir in north-west London, the reservoirs around Heathrow Airport and in the larger ponds and lakes in the Colne Valley, north-east of the city. However, you might pick them up wherever there is calm water along the northern and western edges of the capital.

Another exotic duck which has arrived from foreign quarters - in this case East Asia - is the aptly named **Mandarin Duck**, the male of which is easily the most exquisite-looking duck in Britain today. It has a red bill, orangey whiskers and large, funny orange 'sails' on its back. Mandarins have established relatively healthy breeding numbers across south-east England and some of the best places to see them are Trent Park in Enfield and at some of the ponds and lakes in and around Epping Forest. There are also a few to be found at Bushy Park, Wimbledon Common and at nearby Richmond Park. Anywhere close to the Surrey border is also worth a try. However, if you want a really good view of these beautiful creatures then Kew Gardens is the place to go. A semi-captive population can be found on the lake.

Being beautiful was a dangerous thing for a British bird to be until quite recently. One bird which knew this only too well is the magnificent **Great Crested Grebe**. Huge numbers of them were slaughtered in the mid-nineteenth century for their white breast feathers which were used to make mittens and boas (these are like furry scarves) and their head plumes (another word for feathers), which were used for making hats. All for the fashionable ladies of London! Fortunately a few pairs survived and these handsome birds have spread again across most of the United Kingdom. Go and look for them on almost any London lake or reservoir.

You stand as good a chance of seeing the Great Crested Grebe in Kensington Gardens or Regent's Park in Central London as you do anywhere else. If you go looking in springtime you may be rewarded by seeing mating pairs do their 'waggle dance'. This is where both birds rear up out of the water, chest to chest, and waggle their amazing plumed heads, which look like oriental face masks, at each other.

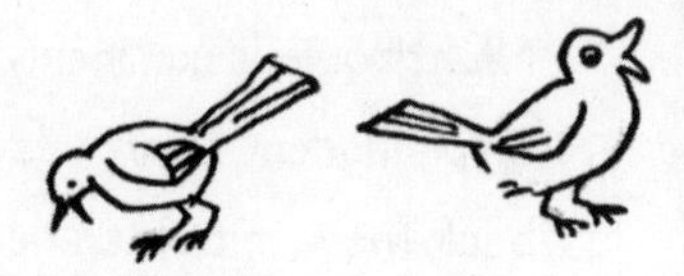

Another avian (bird) that was once the victim of being beautiful - and of having a beautiful song - is the **Goldfinch**. You may have seen these small birds, with their unmistakable red, black and white heads and their gorgeous, golden-yellow wings flashing as they forage for seeding thistle heads or teasel (two of their favourite foods) in the gardens, parks and waste-grounds of the city. Countless thousands of these songsters were captured by greedy traders who would cage them and sell them on the streets of Victorian London to the gentry. It was, I suppose, what you would have had in your home before the radio or CD players were around!

Talking of beautiful singers, have you heard or heard about the song called 'A Nightingale Sang in Berkeley Square'? Probably not, as it was in the music charts a long, long time ago. However, Berkeley Square is in Central London and the

Nightingale is commonly regarded as the finest singer in the bird kingdom. It arrives from Africa in April (and, sadly, goes back there in September) and favours dense, scrubby undergrowth. For this reason it is highly unlikely that one ever sang in Berkeley Square, at least in recent times, but you might just hear one in any of the large parks, gardens or wilder areas away from the centre of the city, where they will pour out their little hearts well into the night (a particularly regular site for them is Bury Wood near Chingford.)

The centre of the city, however, remains home to one of Britain's rarest birds. When bombs destroyed big chunks of London during the Second World War a new habitat (this basically means a home for plants, animals and insects etc.) was formed. Where buildings had previously stood the ground was now just a jumble of rubble. This, alongside the tall sides of buildings that just about remained standing, mimicked pretty closely the natural cliff-face home of the **Black Redstart**. In the whole of the United Kingdom there are thought to be fewer than 100 pairs and London has, perhaps, one third of these. They have been recorded in every borough of the city! One of the more famous places these birds have visited – and even bred in – is the derelict land behind King's Cross Station, where

London's new Channel Tunnel station is being built. But keep your eyes peeled, for the dapper little males (they are prettier than the females, alas) can turn up just about anywhere looking for a mate!

If you want to see something truly outrageous then you are possibly in for a big surprise. London is home to a number of tropically coloured exotic birds. Believe it or not there are a good few thousand **ring-necked** (or **rose-ringed**) **parakeets** flying around Greater London and their numbers are still increasing. These garish flyers are greenish in colour with very long tails and, usually, all red bills. Kew Gardens, Norwood Grove, Hither Green Nature Reserve in Lewisham, near the Rugby Club in Esher and the Wraysbury area in West London are all good places to encounter these Indian settlers. They also have a loud squawk, so with their colouring, you should be able to detect them if they're in the vicinity!

In the north of London you can also find them at Higham's Park in Waltham Forest.

Monk parakeets can be found in small numbers in Borehamwood but they too are expanding in population. If you live near Foots Cray Meadows, in south-east London, or near Lewisham Crematorium, then you may be lucky enough to see **alexandrine parakeets** even though there are probably only a few pairs to be found. Occasionally, **orange-winged amazons** turn up, with one bird recently making a few appearances in Esher. Small numbers of **blue-crowned parakeets** have moved into Bromley and these again are on the increase. All the above are originally descended from escaped cage birds and their numbers are supplemented, now and again, by jail-breaking budgerigars and cockatiels. It may not be long before all of London begins to look like a scene from *The Jungle Book*.

At the opposite end of the colour scale is a bird which is so camouflaged, hiding in dense reed-beds, that it remains one of the least sighted birds in Britain - despite the fact that it is a big bird, related to the Grey Heron. Locating one is not helped by the fact that there is only a handful of pairs in the whole country. In London we are lucky because one nearby site offers perhaps the best opportunity to view these secretive and shy birds in the whole of England. The bird is the curiously named **Bittern** and the place is the famous 'Bittern Watch Hide' at Seventy Acres (Cheshunt Gravel Pit), Fisher's Green in the Lea Valley. These birds arrive for the winter from their breeding sites in Suffolk and a few places elsewhere and can sometimes be found at Amwell Gravel Pits, Wraysbury Gravel Pits in north-west London and a few other places, from time to time, where there is sufficient reed-bed cover. Most excitingly, just as this book was written, three bitterns arrived at the Wetland Centre in Barnes. These birds probably flew in from Holland and it's the nearest bitterns have come to Central London for over 100 years!

Next in line for the 'most secretive bird of the year' might well be the **Water Rail**. This retiring bird looks superficially like the commonplace Moorhen which you can find on just about any pond. The Water Rail, however, is more slender (so he can slip quietly through the reeds and rushes) with a fine, downward-pointed, longish bill. They make the most atrocious noises, during the breeding season, and these sounds have been likened by many to pigs having their throats cut. Although they do breed in London they are more likely to be located during the winter months, when birds fly in from elsewhere, and a glimpse of them may be had as they move from one dense bank of vegetation to another, wherever there is lots of marshy ground. Good places for these birds include all those mentioned above for the Bittern but they can turn up in just about any wet and reedy spot where there is sufficient food and plenty of dense vegetation in which to sneak around.

The new Wetland Centre in Barnes is a good place to go looking for them, and I have watched one only a few paces from the Wildside Hide as it searched around for food.

Whilst you are in any of these places look out too for the **Grey Heron**, which can be very conspicuous, clothed in elegant grey plumage and standing at the water edge with its dagger-like beak ready to stab at any passing frog or newt. Herons occur throughout the city and heronries (think of these like heron cities) are to be found in the high treetops of several London boroughs - in fact, the second largest heronry in the whole country is at Walthamstow Reservoirs in North London. The easiest heronries to observe, however, are in Richmond Park, Battersea Park and Regent's Park in the centre of town.

When most of the birds we have been looking at find a safe place to roost (this is almost like sleeping, but not quite) then a few others sneak out to hunt. Most common amongst these in Greater London is the **Tawny Owl**, which is the one which makes the 'too-whit too-whoo' sound. 'Tawnies' are relatively unafraid of man and you can find them in many of the parks, woods and gardens of the city or wherever there are mature trees for nesting and roosting (Regent's Park is perhaps the most productive central site). When they are nesting, however, you would be wise to stay away from them as they can get pretty angry if they think their young are being threatened (and if you have ever seen an owl's talons you'll know how much damage they could do to you!).

Now less familiar and sadly still largely in decline in south-east England, is the **Barn Owl**. If you've been lucky, you might have seen the owl's ghostly white under-plumage as it's flown past the beam of a car's head-lights. If you are even luckier then you may have watched a day-flying barn owl as it's searched for bank voles in the long grass of a meadow. The county of Essex remains one of the strongholds of this elusive species. Around the area where Essex creeps into London a few pairs still breed, mainly around Rainham Marsh and up in Epping Forest. However, wintering birds may be found hunting the various Thames marshes and other low-lying areas in hard weather.

Little Owls, on the other hand, can be found in a fair number of places around London where grassland and hedgerow are present, although it is not common anywhere. Richmond Park is probably this small owl's nearest home to the city centre. The Little Owl is another of those birds which was introduced into Britain (in the nineteenth century) and in the Midlands and south of England it has fared quite well. This is the owl you are most likely to see in daylight; you might detect its squat little shape sitting defiantly on top of a fence post or tree stump.

Maybe the hardest owl to find in the United Kingdom is the **Long-eared Owl** and in London this bird is largely restricted to a very few winter roosts such as around Northolt, Ickenham and Ramney Marsh. I'm not going to be any more specific about this here as it is important that these birds are left undisturbed. You can often see them hunting in winter, however, over the dry grassland surrounding Walthamstow Reservoirs. The other British owl, the **Short-eared Owl**, can also pitch up in winter-time mainly in those areas with large expanses of flat grassland or marsh. Walthamstow Marshes often holds a few wintering birds and Rainham Marshes, in East London, is one of the most reliable winter sites for these birds in the entire United Kingdom.

Recently, however, one owl in Central London put all the others in the shade (quite literally) and that was the escaped and quite immense **Eagle Owl**. This massive owl, quite capable of taking a cat home for dinner, frequented the Central London Parks for a couple of years, but was sadly found dead at St Paul's Cathedral, believed to have dined on a poisoned pigeon.

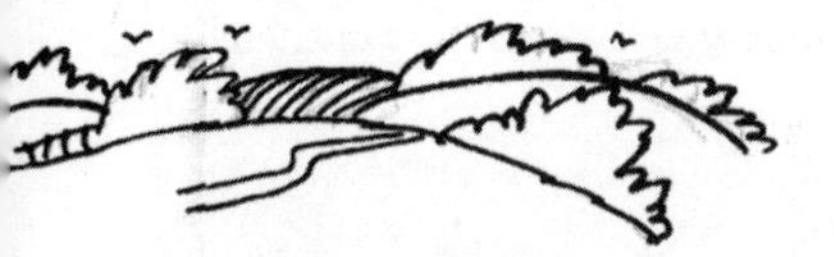

Go to any large park or area of woodland in London and you have a good chance of spying a **Great Spotted Woodpecker**. In fact, if you have a garden with lots of trees then you may be able to tempt these lovely black, white and bright red birds to take fat and other high-energy foods from a bird feeder. These birds are currently increasing in London and occur even in the middle of town in places such as Kensington Gardens, Hyde Park, Battersea Park, Holland Park and Regent's Park. Its smaller cousin, the **Lesser Spotted Woodpecker**, has similar colouring but is much shyer and much less common. They are usually to be found in the tree tops in the more secluded London woodlands (and very rarely in the central parks).

Much more obvious is the **Green Woodpecker**, which flicks out its long, sticky tongue in search of ants in the short grass of many of London's parks and other similar spaces. The Green Woodpecker is a relatively large bird and you might hear it 'laughing' from a nearby tree or on the ground, before you catch sight of it. Clapham Common sometimes affords good views of this brightly plumaged bird and they can now be seen in many of the central parks where the Great Spotted Woodpecker hangs out (the Green Woodpecker has also been increasing and has started to live 'down-town' in recent years).

Just catching sight of the brilliantly feathered **Kingfisher** is about all most people can manage. If you're lucky, you'll see a dash of metallic blue as the bird speeds down the river. Despite its brilliant coloration the Kingfisher is a very hard bird to discover as it sits on a branch above the water waiting to dive down and spear a minnow or other small fish. Kingfishers need clean, clear water and a sandy bank nearby in which to excavate their tunnelled nests. In Greater London there is a surprising number of places which still satisfy the Kingfisher's needs. You can find them very close in to the centre of the city and they do appear, from time to time, at the lakes of the central parks and on Regent's Canal. The rivers, reservoirs and lakes around the perimeter of London still offer the best opportunity to observe these jewel-like birds.

To include all the birds which occur in London (there are over 300 species recorded) would take a much bigger book than this but I hope the above examples of the wonderful birds which do make their homes (or take their holidays) in the capital will tempt you to read more.

I could easily have talked about Europe's smallest bird, the Firecrest, or its brother, the Goldcrest. I could have mentioned the massively beaked Hawfinch (sadly declining fast but still around in reasonable numbers in Epping Forest) or talked about the Jay, which is shy in the countryside (where it is known as 'the watcher of the woods') but pretty bold in many parts of London, where it often shares the contents of a bin bag with the Fox. Swifts, swallows and martins would also have featured.

The magnificent Golden Pheasant, which lives a semi-wild existence in Kew Gardens, might even have been sneaked in. We might also have considered the tube-travelling pigeons of the Circle Line. Cuckoos, collared doves, waxwings and pied flycatchers all come to mind but you will have to do more reading elsewhere to find out more (a very good book, although it is mainly intended for serious adult birdwatchers, is called *Where to Watch Birds in the London Area*, and it is published by Helm).

Chapter Two

Hoofs, Tusks and Antlers
The Mammals of London

One of the first animals which comes to my mind when thinking about London is the **Black Rat**.It was this furry creature that provided a nice home for the flea which brought the Black Death to England. It is generally agreed that this 'pest' arrived in the boats of returning Crusaders in the thirteenth century. Surely it is strange, then, that this rodent is now one of Britain's rarest animals - with a population around 1500. The Port of London is one of the last places where this animal exists in the United Kingdom.

So what brought about the demise of this pestilence-carrying creature? Almost certainly it was its relative, the **Brown Rat**, probably arriving from Russia - again in boats - in the early eighteenth century, which pushed out the Black Rat. The Brown Rat is a bigger and more aggressive animal (some have been seen that are as big as rabbits). Brown rats are now the most common animals by far in London with a population estimated to be around 10 million. Despite many attempts to control their numbers the Brown Rat has confounded the best plans and many now feed on the poisons laid down for them with no ill effect! There are healthy numbers (some may say unhealthy numbers) in the London sewers and in the Underground system. In the streets, late at night, these rats are attracted to wherever there are restaurants that leave their rubbish unprotected! Beware, though, for it's said that brown rats will jump up and bite you on the throat if you corner them and they certainly carry some nasty diseases.

Still down in the Underground system you will often see small, black mice scurrying between the tracks at many Tube stations (but make very sure you are well back from the platform edge if you want to see these - there is no point losing your head for the rats to feed upon!). These little creatures are the same animals which inhabit nearly every building in London, the **House Mouse**. They are certainly different in colour from the variety which lives behind the skirting board and it's possible they may be evolving into a separate sub-species.

Many of the old Underground tunnels, together with other cave-like structures and hollow trees, provide home and shelter to what some people describe as 'flying mice'. These are, of course, the bats. Londoners are particularly fortunate in hosting nine different species of **Bat**. Most common of these is the tiny **Pipistrelle Bat** (it has recently been discovered that there are three different species of Pipistrelle in the United Kingdom but that is too complicated to go into here). It roosts mainly in the roof spaces of houses. They come out at night wherever there are sufficient insects to feed upon in the city. One of the largest bats you are likely to encounter in Greater London is the **Serotine Bat**, which tends to favour mature parks, on the outskirts of London (particularly in the southern boroughs), where it may be seen to chase the larger flying beetles to the ground before eating them.

There is one bat which is even bigger (if only by a small amount) and that is the **Noctule Bat**. This is often the first bat to emerge in the evening and will often appear before the sun has completely gone down. This bat needs tree holes (it often uses old woodpecker holes) to roost in so there is no point looking for them where these don't exist. However, you can find them right in the heart of the city in Regent's Park and Hyde Park.

Other places you can go looking for them are Wimbledon Common, Beddingon Park, South Norwood Country Park, Oxleas

Wood (Greenwich), Hampstead Heath, Osterley Park, the Wetlands Centre (Barnes), Hollow Pond (Waltham Forest) and Wanstead Flats (Redbridge).

If you see a bat flying low over a park pond then you can be quite sure it will be a **Daubenton's Bat** sweeping up unsuspecting insects. Again all the above, except Oxleas Wood, are regular haunts of this bat but you can also find them at Bushy Park in Richmond. The **Natterer's Bat** can be found in Highgate Wood and in the gardens around Chiswick House but perhaps the most difficult bat to locate (even if you know how to identify them - and that usually requires a special instrument which measures the high-pitched noises that bats make) is the **Brown Long-eared Bat**. As its name suggests, the Brown Long-eared has very big ears (which are nearly as long as its body!). It sneaks out when it's very dark and rarely strays from cover. Lucky observers have found them at Wimbledon Common and Bushy Park (though I don't recommend you go looking for them all alone!). You would be more than lucky to stumble upon the other species of bat in London as they are very rare. They include the **Whiskered Bat**, **Brandt's Bat** and **Leisler's Bat** (these are present in Highgate Wood).

Remember, though, if you want to see bats don't go looking for them in winter when they are hibernating (think of this as one very long lie-in).

If big is what mainly interests you then they don't come bigger, in London, than the various species of **Deer** to be found in the city's parks and quieter places. Deer have had a long history in the capital with, in days past, the king or queen alone determining who could hunt these royal beasts. Many of the deer which survive in the old royal parks are directly descended from these animals. The most attractive of these is certainly the **Fallow Deer**, which you are most likely to encounter in Richmond Park. However their numbers are greatly reduced from the 1600 animals which roamed the park up to the beginning of the twentieth century. To get a really close view, take a trip to Alexandra Park where a small captive herd are to be found.

The other large deer living in the capital is the **Red Deer,** which still finds a place to live in Richmond Park.

By far the most unusual - and peculiar-looking - deer to be found in Greater London is the **Chinese Muntjac Deer**, which is a small dog-sized deer with rather ferocious-looking tusks. England and Wales are the only places in Europe where these animals exist and they established themselves here after having escaped from the Duke of Woburn's Estate in Bedfordshire, in the late nineteenth century. They have been spreading ever since and are certainly now breeding in North London (especially around Trent Park in Enfield and Scratch Wood in Barnet. They've also been sighted as close to the city centre as North Wood in Haringey and at Alexandra Park.

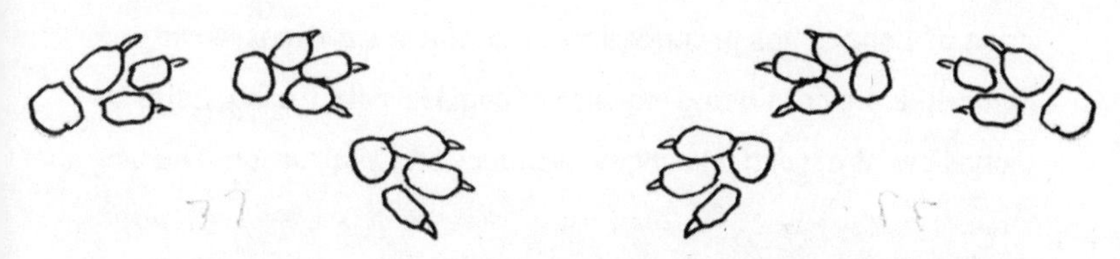

More recent (and rather more scary) escapees include the **Wild Boar** and while they have not yet been seen in Greater London there is a healthy breeding population nearby in the Kent Weald. In the Great Storm of 1987 some animals escaped from local farms and they have been increasing in number and spreading ever since - it may not be long before this secretive forest-dweller returns to some of its former haunts in the south London boroughs (the last English boars were probably to be found in Windsor Great Park, in the early seventeenth century, where they were hunted by King James I).

Do you like being really scared? If the answer is no then you will probably want to skip the next section.

A number of places in London are said to have 'Big Cats' roaming around. Whilst most reports of escaped pumas and other large wild felines are hoaxes or mis-identifications, there is no doubt that the occasional escaped animals does survive in the wild for long periods - perhaps even breeding. The western edge of London has produced most of these sightings, with Puma-like big cats being reported from Harrow, Ealing, Esher, Hounslow, Watford, Haringey, Sunbury and Walton-on-Thames.

And if you want hard evidence: in 1975 a **Black Leopard** cub which had escaped (perhaps from private ownership) was re-captured in East Peckham!

Feral cats, on the other hand, can be encountered just about anywhere in the city. These are the offspring of domestic cats which have decided to leave home and live in the wild. Although their parents may be domesticated, these are genuinely wild animals and they are just as wary as real wild cats.

Ratty's True Identity

One animal that has long been a favourite for generations of children is Ratty from *The Wind in the Willows*, a lovely book by Kenneth Grahame about a group of creatures living along and nearby a river. In fact Ratty is a slightly confusing name, as he is really a **Water Vole**. Water voles have sadly been disappearing from many of the United Kingdom's rivers (not at the hands of the **Weasel**, who are the baddies in *The Wind in the Willows*) but largely from the aggressive antics of the

American Mink. These rather bullying creatures escaped from fur farms or were released by animal activists in the middle of the twentieth century. I'm afraid that, although these activists probably thought they were doing the right thing in releasing these animals, the mink have wreaked havoc on other species of wildlife that are native to Britain. The natural habitat of the Mink is by water and due to their vicious nature, they have quickly spread throughout the United Kingdom's river systems. Sadly, this (together with habitat loss, disturbance and pollution) have left the Water Vole in the terrible position of being Britain's fastest disappearing animal.

However, while the American Mink can be found right in the heart of London, the Water Vole is with any luck on the brink of recovery in the capital. One of the places which is at the forefront of trying to re-introduce 'Ratty' to the wild is the newly created Wetlands Centre at Barnes in West London, where around 100 animals have recently been released. This is a great place to visit if you are interested in wildlife. Elsewhere, the Water Vole can still be found in small pockets in the boroughs around the edges of the city and has recently even been recorded in Alexandra Park. Two of the best spots to catch sight of them are at the London Wildlife Trust Reserves at Crane Park Island and at the Chase in Enfield. And good news - a recent survey of Rainham Marshes suggests that there is a much larger population of water voles here than had previously been thought.

There is probably no animal easier to see in London than the **Grey Squirrel**. Most of us will think of this apparently charming, bushy-tailed creature as a friendly, ingenious and rather nosy inhabitant who will appear wherever there is sufficient tree cover. They are far from friendly, however, to much of the resident bird populations (whose eggs they steal and eat) or to the original, native British squirrel, the **Red Squirrel**.

Unfortunately you will not find this rather more pretty and smaller squirrel in London - or indeed much of the British Isles - today as it has found it hard to compete with the more robust **Grey Squirrel**. It is largely unproven, however, that greys will fight with reds. The Grey Squirrel was introduced in many parts of England, towards the end of the nineteenth century, but it is probably the animals that were let loose in Regent's Park,

Richmond Park and Woburn Park are the ancestors of today's London squirrels.

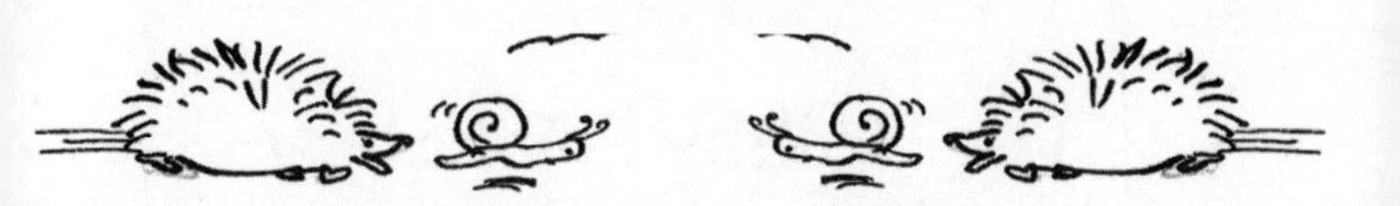

If there is a favourite amongst the London animal kingdom then my own daughter would certainly vote in the **Hedgehog**, despite the fact it is perhaps the least cuddly on account of its spines! If you go out with a torch in the summer months, once it gets dark, of course, and search around your garden (if you are lucky enough to have one) then you may well be rewarded with seeing a hedgehog or two dining out on slugs and snails. They are great friends of the gardener!

You can find hedgehogs just about anywhere in the city, as long as there is somewhere for them to hibernate. They like big piles of dead leaves or sticks and logs – so check your bonfire before you set light to it! Many people will put out cat food to feed their local hedgehogs but don't put out milk and bread as they find these foods hard to digest and they have little 'energy value'. You can make barriers to stop them falling into garden ponds or from wandering into the road, which is where the hedgehog often meets a flattened end! In fact, being in London is great for hedgehog-spotting as there are more of them here

(Highgate Cemetery is a favourite spot) than there are in much of the surrounding countryside.

The Healthy Fox Eatery

Today Only

- Old Chicken Carcass Throw-away
- Fish Bone and Carrot Peel Stew
- Eggshell and Bird Seed Medley
- Bacon Rind Sandwich
- Specials
- Big Bowl of Earth Worms

After the Hedgehog and the Grey Squirrel, the animal you are most likely to see in Greater London is the **Red Fox**. If you are in a car in the evening you may see out of the window quite a few of these wild dogs – especially in the leafy suburbs. However, they can be seen right in the heart of the city (they have even been seen strolling down Piccadilly). A recent survey of what foxes eat (and no, they didn't ask the foxes, silly) revealed that their diet includes a thrown-away, city-centre favourite - the Chinese take-away!

Like the Hedgehog, there are likely to be more foxes currently in London than you will find in the country around the city's suburbs. The best places to spot them include Chigwell, Hornchurch and Finchley, in north London, and Carshalton, Coulsdon, Purley and Beckenham, south of the city.

Of a similar size, but much less likely to be tracked down, is the **Badger** (he's another character in Kenneth Grahame's *The Wind in the Willows*). Epping Forest and Richmond Park are among the favourite London places for these nocturnal animals ('nocturnal' is simply another word for a creature which comes out at night). Badgers need undisturbed woodland to breed and they often spread along railway embankments (and you are definitely not allowed to go looking for them there!). This is because railway lines often provide undisturbed green space which may join various woods and other habitats together. Sadly many badgers are killed by passing trains. They are also unfortunately killed by cars on the roads of Britain. Contrary to popular belief, the Badger does not hibernate but, if the weather gets really cold, then it will stay warm and cosy in its 'sett' (the underground chambers which they dig to live in) until the temperature rises. If you do find a sett be very careful who you tell as there are still some bad people who hunt them with dogs for what they call 'sport'.

Would it surprise you to learn that a **Bottlenose Dolphin** was seen swimming in the Thames between Blackfriar's Bridge and Wapping (where it was later and sadly found dead) during mid-summer in 2001? With only two populations in the entire United Kingdom - one in Scotland and one in Wales - it is a rare event for a Bottlenose Dolphin to turn up in London. This appearance must, in small part, be explained by the cleaning up of the river (it wasn't long ago when most of the river in London was 'dead' - but more of this later). Other 'marine' mammals (meaning 'sea-living') which are found in the Thames estuary include the **harbour seals** (these are sometimes also called **common seals**) and **grey seals**, but just how far up the river they are likely to venture remains to be seen.

From the other end of the Thames we can hope that the **Otter** will, once again, return to the city. Under careful conservation and re-introductions these big and muscular river animals are beginning to re-establish themselves in the upper Thames. In London we have not had the privilege of seeing wild otters in London for many years, although in 1922 there was magazine report of otters playing under Westminster Bridge!

Certainly otters existed, in small numbers, in the lower river (and in the Lea Valley, the Colne Valley and rivers Stort and Mole) as late as the 1940s. The last London breeding site was probably the Essex and Middlesex Filter Beds in Waltham Forest. However, a new threat may be about to strike at these lovable animals in the form of a virus, which has been discovered in the Mink population in the upperThames and can be spread to otters.

A similar mammal, which disappeared from the British fauna (this is a Latin world for animals) is the **European Beaver**, which, as well as being re-introduced at a remote site in Scotland, is being used by the Kent Wildlife Trust to graze their Ham Fen Nature Reserve on the River Stour - not far from the capital.

If you look at a painting of one of the great kings and queens of England, you will often find that they are wearing a most beautiful white animal fur as part of their elaborate costume. This is 'ermine' and was a most treasured luxury. Judges began to wear it too because the soft, white fur was associated with purity and honesty.

Ermine comes from the white, winter-phase of the **Stoat** and although you won't find any white stoats in London (they only turn white in the colder, mountainous parts of Britain), they can be found in most areas where their dinner is abundant. A stoat's 'dinner' is almost exclusively rabbit and when the country's rabbits almost died out, as a result of Myxomatosis in the 1950s, then stoat numbers fell dramatically. Myxomatosis was transmitted from rabbit to rabbit by a kind of flea, which required the warmth of the rabbit burrow to thrive. As some rabbits began to live above ground then the flea became less of a problem and rabbit numbers began to climb once again. This of course meant that stoats were able to begin building up their numbers again.

It might also interest you to know that rabbits are also an introduced species, and were probably brought here by the Romans. So perhaps there are more stoats around now than there were historically. Wimbledon Common is a good spot to go looking for them.

The Stoat's near, but smaller, relative is the **Weasel** and is possibly easier to discover in London because its main prey are small rodents and there are more of these around the city than there are rabbits. For their size, weasels are among nature's most ferocious hunters and they will often go in search of their victims in family gangs. No doubt it was observing this behaviour that led Kenneth Grahame to give weasels the part of the baddies in *The Wind in the Willows.*

Of course, the above does not cover all the mammals of London - I have left out various species of mice, voles and shrews and the Hare and the Polar Bear (only kidding!). More can be discovered by doing some of your own research. Some of the websites at the back of this book will help you on your way!

Chapter Three

Damsels, Dragons and Creepy Crawlies

The Insects and Invertebrates of London

Have you ever seen a **Stag Beetle**? If you haven't, and you live in London, then you are in one of the best places in Europe to put things right. It is really quite a rare beetle and globally threatened (this means it is getting rarer nearly everywhere on Earth where it occurs). However, the stag beetle has been recorded in nearly every London borough.

So what does it look like? Quite unmistakable! For one thing it is the largest ground-living beetle in Britain and can reach a length of 8 centimetres (about as long as your biggest finger) but they are usually about half that size. The other very obvious thing about the Stag Beetle is the thing that gives it its name - its 'antlers'. Although in appearance they are just like a stag deer's antlers, they are, in fact, huge 'mandibles' (this means mouth parts, and they are bigger in the male than in the female). These look pretty scary but it is the female's much smaller jaws which will give you the most powerful nip!

What stag beetles need is lots of dead and decaying wood in which to lay their eggs and in which the emerging grubs can live before they mature into adult beetles. You can imagine that tidy parkland is not the best place to go looking for them. The south and west of London provides the best chance of a sighting. Wherever woodland occurs in Richmond, Beckenham, Dulwich and Wandsworth is your best bet but you can also find them in the north-east boroughs, especially around Epping Forest. The best time of year to see them is between the months of May and June, when the adults emerge from hiding.

If you don't get lucky with the above you might uncover, with a bit of poking around, a **Lesser Stag Beetle** which, although smaller than the Stag Beetle, is still a very impressive insect. You can find these just about anywhere in the city where suitable habitat exists. It has similar requirements to its bigger cousin, so you might get lucky and see them both!

In terms of size, the next largest ground beetle you are likely to encounter is the **Devil's Coach Horse**. This beetle is also well named because it is quite the most gruesome-looking thing, like some long, dark creature from the Underworld. In fact the underworld is where it likes to live – under stones and logs in gardens and hedgerows, just about anywhere.

London is home to some other rare beetles besides the Stag Beetle. One of the **Chafer Beetle** family was recently discovered in the Adelaide Road Nature Reserve, in Camden, having not been recorded in the country since the 1950s. In

Richmond Park we have one of the best sites in Britain for rare beetles, boasting over a quarter of all known British beetle species. **Musk beetles** are present in Wimbledon Common and Putney Common and the nationally rare **Jewel Beetle** is hanging on in Haringey's Bluebell Wood. The London Wildlife Trust (LWT) Reserve at Denham Lock Wood in north-west London is a prime spot for the bright red **Cardinal Beetle** (another one that is well named - what colour do cardinals wear?). The **Bloody-nosed Beetle** is black and although its name would suggest it's got a red nose, it actually comes from the fact that if you disturb it, it will spit out a bloody red liquid. This beetle is pretty large and is quite common throughout London so you shouldn't have too much trouble tracking one down.

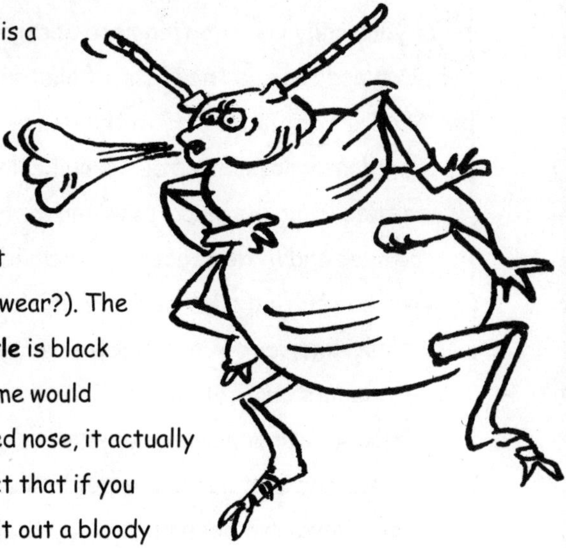

Beetles are not restricted to dry land, of course, and some of the most dramatic can be found on a pond-dipping expedition. **The Great Diving Beetle** is a large and fierce predator (something which hunts down and kills its prey) and you might net one of these in any clean and weedy pond or ditch. I am not sure where you might find the even larger **Great Silver Beetle** (they can get to be as big as Stag Beetles), as they are now nationally scarce and are only to be found in southern England.

If you really want to find rare beetles then the best place to go is the **Natural History Museum**. No, I am not referring to the dead specimens pinned into glass cases but genuine, live foreign beetles living in the carpets and in the cracks, crevices and little spaces in the building itself. Here you can find such wonderfully named insects as the **American Wasp Beetle** and the United Kingdom's only colony (so far!) of **Asian odd beetles** (I wonder what makes them odd?). The Science and Victoria and Albert Museums next door have also been invaded by the likes of **Guernsey beetles** and **brown carpetbeetles**. It remains to be seen if these unwelcome visitors can be successfully eradicated.

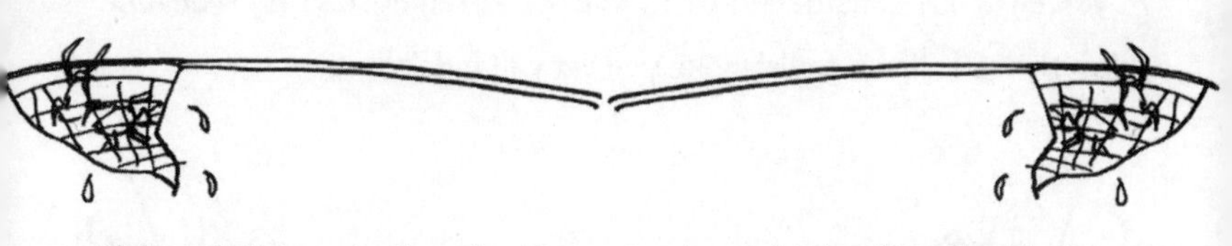

Although it is not a beetle, the water bug which will probably give you the biggest fright is the **Water Scorpion** with its huge, pincer-like front legs which it uses to hunt down small fish, tadpoles and suchlike. Be careful if you handle this bug as it can give you quite a sharp bite! Again you can catch one of these in your net in any clean, weedy pond in the city. You may also be fortunate enough to scoop out a **Water Stick Insect** - looking for all the world like a preying mantis (and nearly as long!). If you do net one, though, be sure to put it back where you found it.

Talking of water scorpions, do you know that real scorpions are related to spiders? And did you know that there are some knocking around parts of London? Well, there are!

If you go down to the docks today be sure of a big surprise, for in Ongar and at Tilbury and Sheerness, on the Thames Estuary, there are thriving colonies of **European Yellow-tailed Scorpions**. As with some of the other arrivals to the United Kingdom that we have talked about earlier, it travelled here by ship. I'm afraid I have to be very strict here, however, and warn you not to go searching for these dangerous creatures in the nooks and crannies where they like to hide out. Although their venom is not considered to be life-threatening, a sting from one of these fellows could make you very ill indeed!

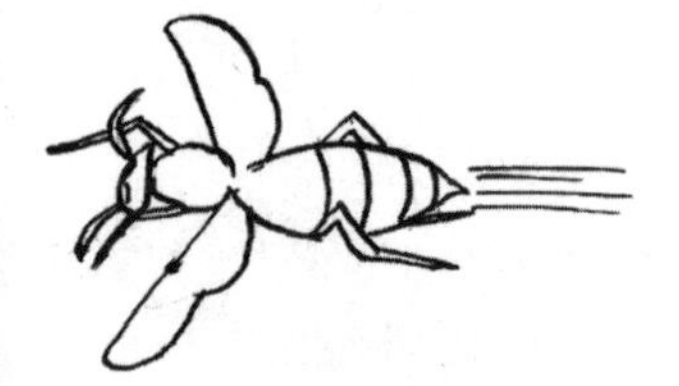

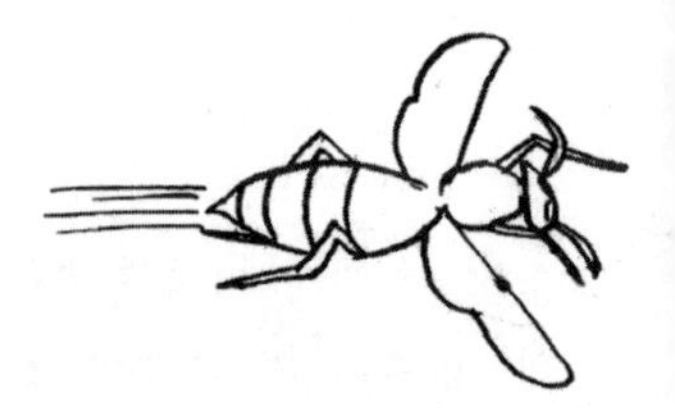

Another species whose sting is best avoided is the **Hornet**. This is our biggest wasp and is around 30 millimetres in length (about twice the size of the wasps you are more familiar with). Wherever woodland exists, with dead trees providing nest sites, these impressive insects might be discovered, but they are relatively uncommon only in the Greater London area.

If there is one insect that you don't want to see, what would it be? Chances are it would be the **Cockroach**, which runs around the skirting boards and behind the sinks of so many homes, hospitals and public buildings in London today. Cockroaches are one of the most ancient living things and their fossils have been left in rocks that are over 250 million years old! There are a number of different species existing in Britain, some of which are native and outdoor-living.

The most common house cockroaches living in London, however, are the **German Cockroach** and the **Oriental Cockroach** (but other types are around too!). As well as being dirty and disease-carrying, cockroaches are also cannibals. In fact, cockroaches will eat just about anything, and there is a gruesome story that a sleeping family of children awoke one morning to find that cockroaches had eaten their eyebrows! So, if you do find one, report it immediately to an adult who can contact the pest control people.

While we're on the subject of unsavoury members of London's insect population, there is something which has only recently been recognized as a separately evolved species. This one bites and it lives exclusively in the London Underground system and - although this might sound unbelievable - it is genetically different from Tube line to tube line (genetic is just a posh word which sort of means the particular ingredients that go to make up an animal).

What is it, then? It's a **Mosquito**. So a Central Line mosquito might will be different from a Northern Line mosquito! It has been down there, evolving away since at least the Second World War. They draw their bloody meals mainly from the mice, rats and pigeons which you find down in the Underground but they also consider humans to be an occasional treat ...

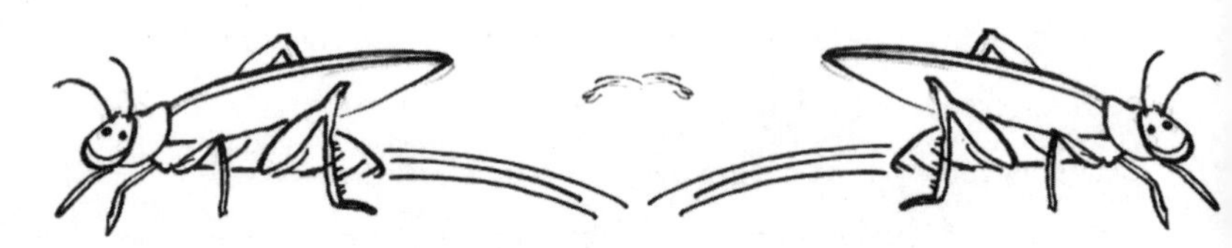

Crickets and **Grasshoppers** not only occur within the M25 orbital motorway but, in some places, they thrive and there are even some pretty rare specimens among their numbers. One of the most special is the **Roesel's Bush Cricket**, a species which has been slowly spreading up from the south coast of England and which you can find on Wimbledon Common, Hither Green Nature Reserve (Lewisham), Yeading Brook Meadows Reserve (Hillingdon) and many other London parks and meadows, even in the centre.

Another species of cricket which has been spreading northwards is the **Long-winged Conehead** and these can be searched for in many of the same places you will find the Roesel's Bush Cricket.

Special grasshoppers include the **Stripe-winged Grasshopper**, the song of which has been likened to a police siren. This is quite rare but has recently been discovered at Putney Common and the London Wildlife Trust's reserves at Camley Street and Adelaide Road in Camden.

Our largest **Bush Cricket**, at almost 50 millimetres in length, is the **Great Green Bush Cricket** and the best place to go looking for these is in patches of scrubland, particularly on the southern edge of Greater London.

There are even **House Crickets** reported occasionally, from some of the larger, well-heated buildings in the city. These arrivals originate from Africa and can only live indoors in Britain except in very warm weather - one long-established colony exists wild at London Zoo. If you don't locate any of the above, don't give up because there are a good many more Cricket and Grasshopper species alive and well in the capital.

The Trials of Miss Muffett

Spiders are perhaps less attractive than grasshoppers to most people but they are even more fascinating. The daughter of one sixteenth-century London public figure, the Reverend Doctor Thomas Muffett (and we all know who she was, don't we?) was on the receiving end of her father's rather eccentric experiments.

It's no wonder Miss Muffet was frightened away - her dad got some spiders to bite her, to test for unfortunate reactions. It was lucky for Miss Muffett that there aren't any poisonous spiders in the country!

However, you too might be frightened away by the second largest spider in the United Kingdom, which is common wherever there is somewhere to cast its massive web in the city. One of them lives outside my living room window and its web stretches a good three feet across! This **Garden Spider** does not have a 'common name' (this is the non-scientific name we give to plants and animals) but its Latin name is 'Araneus quadratus' and its grotesque, swollen round body alone can reach 20 millimeters across. Thankfully they hide away in winter!

One of the most amazing of the capital's spiders is the **Purse-web Spider**, which does not spin a web but lives in a hole in the ground, cocooned in a silken tube. When the spider 'feels' an insect walking overhead it thrusts its big, scary fangs at the unfortunate prey and sucks it down into its den to be eaten.

Maybe the spider which we are all most familiar with, as every one of us will have some living in our homes, is the ferocious-looking **House Spider**. This is the one you might sometimes find trapped in the bottom of the bath. However, don't be scared for it is quite harmless and will return you the favour of saving its life by catching flying insects around the home.

Seven Stunning Spidery Facts

- Spiders are not insects but are related to ticks and scorpions

- The silk thread which spiders make is stronger than steel of the same thickness!

- Spiders can travel for many miles in the air by spinning a long silk thread which is caught in the wind

- Many female spiders eat their unfortunate partners after mating with them

- Spiders do not have jaws but poisonous fangs just in front of their mouths

- The largest British spider is the **Swamp** (or **Raft**) **Spider**, which can dive under water to hunt for small fish and which has a bite which is mildly poisonous to humans

- One of the most curious British spiders is the **Zebra Spider** which has black and white stripes and which can jump up vertical surfaces!

Less than harmless (though of little danger to Man) are the **tarantulas** which are very occasionally reported from the docks of London. They have arrived here in boats, of course. But these are unlikely to survive long as they are principally bird-eating and cannot tolerate our cold weather.

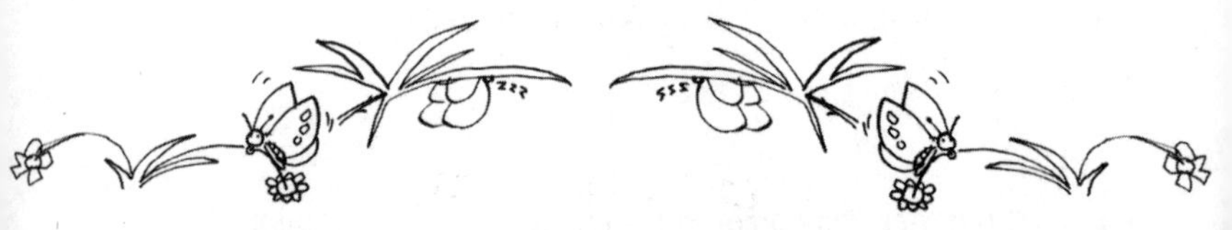

For sheer beauty in the world of insects we must turn to the butterflies and moths which grace London with their presence. Some of the best places to search out butterflies are the London Wildlife Trust reserves at Gunnersby Triangle, Battersea Park and West Kent Golf Course in Bromley, which can boast recording 28 species, including the rare **Small Blue**! Another excellent butterfly spot is Alexandra Park, in Haringey, which comes in not far behind the last site in having noted 24 species. If you want to know where some of the other scarcer 'flutter-bys' live, then check out Wimbledon and Putney Commons, where you can encounter the **White-letter Hairstreak** and the **Purple Hairstreak** (which can also be found at Bramley Park in Croydon and around the Warren Pond in Waltham Forest).

However, one of the most special was at Putney in the summer of 2001 when the very uncommon **Adonis Blue** turned up .

The **Brown Argus** can be tracked down at the Birdbrook Road Reserve, in Greenwich, where you can also discover the **Common Blue** and the **Holly Blue**. The latter is also present in Knight's Hill Wood, Lambeth, as is the Speckled Wood, which also haunts the Rectory Lane Pond in Bexley. Other good sites include Yeading Brook Meadows (Hillingdon) and Totteridge Fields (Barnet) where you may chance upon **skippers**, **gatekeepers** and all the more common - but nonetheless spectacular - types such as **Painted Lady**, **Peacock**, **Red Admiral** or **Small Tortoiseshell**.

For moths, you will generally need to go out at night with a torch but there are daytime flying species and the dazzling **5-spot Burnet**, with its metallic black-green wings splashed with bright red spots, can be seen at most of the sites listed above (for butterflies). Many of the **Hawkmoth** family can be found in the right habitats in Greater London and for size, these are amongst the most dramatic of all British insects. The **Privet Hawkmoth**, for example, is a staggering 100 millimeters across its wings (almost as large as a 10-year-old child's hand).

However it is the day-flying, migrant **Hummingbird Hawkmoth** which is perhaps the most noteworthy, making appearances on Wimbledon and Putney Commons and at Broxbourne Woods in North London. It has a wingspan of around 45 millimeters - still pretty big!

Remember, though, that there is little point looking for butterflies and moths in the winter - they are fast asleep.

If size is what counts, then few things in the British insect world can compare with some of the **dragonflies**. The most obvious places to go hunting these impressive creatures is close to the ponds and lakes which they need to breed in, but because they are fantastic fliers they can be found some long distances away from the nearest suitable water source.

Almost top of the 'huge' league (it is just beaten by the **Golden-ringed Dragonfly**, which would be a most rare site in London) is the **Emperor Dragonfly**. This grand creature clocks in with a body length of nearly 80 millimetres. The best places to find this giant is at what is probably London's best dragonfly venue - Wimbledon Common, where an incredible 14 species have been racked up! Here you will also meet the massive **brown** and **southern hawkers** and the fat, chalk-blue (the male that is) **Broad-bodied Chaser**. It may not be long before the Wetland Centre at Barnes begins to match the Wimbledon total.

Alexandra Park, Haringey, is another choice place to visit for these dragonflies. Other prime sites are Cornhill Meadows (Waltham Abbey), Staines and Stanwell Moors, Dulwich Park and Lea Valley Country Park. If you want to 'go central', try out the small wildlife area of the Natural History Museum!

During your pond-dipping expedition you may have dredged out a most hideous and bloodthirsty-looking beast. Chances are that you have captured a **Dragonfly Nymph** (or young). These scary-looking things are amongst the most vicious of all underwater predators, hunting down even quite decent-sized fish fry and other unfortunate pond dwellers. Do put them back, though, as they will soon emerge from their ugly coats and transform themselves into the glamorous adults that we have been talking about.

Damselflies come in many different forms too and, although generally smaller than their dragonfly neighbors, they can be just as spectacularly painted - many with shining, metallic bodies. If you want to be able to tell a dragonfly and a damselfly apart, wait until they land and look at the way they settle their wings. A dragonfly will hold its wings out so that the animal appears like a cross shape, and a damselfly hold its wings along its body like a stick.

As before, this section of the book could have been much, much longer but it is well worth sneaking in one intriguing little creature at the end. It's the **Glow Worm**. This fascinating creature emits its greenish light on summer nights on some of the capital's commons and woodland rides. Maybe the best area to go looking is along the southern edge of London's outer boroughs (but remember to take an adult with you!).

CHAPTER FOUR

Slitherers, Sliders and Hoppy Things

London's Reptiles and Amphibians

Snakes in London? Surely not, I hear you say. But there are - though it would be wrong to say that they are common or widespread.

The United Kingdom's only poisonous snake, the **Adder** (sometimes called the **Northern Viper**), is our only potentially dangerous land animal. In fact it is very hard to get bitten at all because snakes are extremely sensitive creatures and have usually slithered away long before you can get anywhere near them! Most bites occur when someone stupidly tries to pick them up or when they are trodden on accidentally. Nevertheless, it is wise (if you're lucky enough to encounter one) never to get too close to an adder. It is quite a thick snake and reaches a length of around 60 centimetres but

some have been seen that are almost a metre long (quite big, when you consider a five-year-old child is on average almost that height).

Adders can appear in a variety of different colours - from grey to creamy yellow to reddish-brown - but what makes them distinctive is the dark, zig-zaggy line which runs down along their backs.

Snakes hibernate in the winter and emerge on warm days in springtime to raise their temperatures (because they are cold-blooded). Male adders will fight with each other (when they are both interested in the same female adder!) and these wrestling matches can get quite angry and noisy with lots of hissing. All the counties in the south-east of England have Adder populations. The best places you're likely to find them, however, are in those areas south of the city that are rich in woodland rides and chalk downlands.

The only other snake you are likely to meet in London (though there are other species in Britain) is the even larger **Grass Snake**. This animal, which is completely harmless (unless you are a frog or a small fish being pursued as lunch), can grow to be up to a metre long - in the case of the female - and the biggest one ever found in the United Kingdom was nearly twice that long!

There is a little clue above as to what kind of habitat grass snakes prefer to live in. Like most animals, it likes to be not too far away from where it can find an easy meal (we're just the same, aren't we?) and, in this case, that happens to be near water. In fact you are more likely to see a grass snake swimming than you are to see one on solid ground. They can pitch up just about anywhere in the city providing there is water with a healthy stock of amphibians and fish fry, some cover (in which to hide out) and somewhere to lay their eggs. They need somewhere warm for this like a compost or a manure heap. Wimbledon Common has a few grass snakes (adders have been sighted here too), as have the Essex and Middlesex Filter Beds in Waltham Forest. The new Wetlands Centre in Barnes looks like a perfect home for grass snakes although I am not sure if they have been recorded there as yet.

Now and again some rather more frightening animals like **boa constrictors**, **king snakes** or **garter snakes** escape and survive wild for a while but these are usually re-captured quickly (in the case of the larger specimens) or they succumb to the harsh British winter.

Fangs for letting me know!

- Snakes shed their skins every year in order to grow bigger

- The Adder, Britain's only poisonous snake, rarely bites man and only then when it is provoked. However, around 100 people a year are bitten in the UK but there have been no reported deaths for many years

- Grass snakes can stay under water for up to 30 minutes when searching for prey

- Snakes' jaws dislocate (the top and bottom jaws can disconnect) so that they can swallow quite large animals. The unfortunate creature is then swallowed whole and can live for some time inside the snake while it is slowly digested.

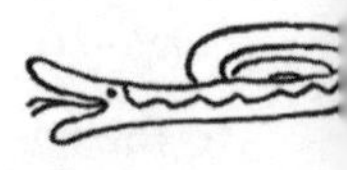

When is a snake not a snake? When it's a **Slow Worm**, of course! Although they look just like snakes, slow worms are, in fact, legless lizards. For lizards they can grow to an astonishing size with the biggest one ever recorded in the United Kingdom reaching almost half a metre long! Generally, they are only around half that size and are very smooth to the touch with almost metallic-looking, reddish-brown through to silvery-grey skins. Should you stumble across one please don't try to catch it as it may shed its tail in an effort to escape. The Slow Worm's favourite foods are snails, slugs and worms and for this reason they are more widespread than snakes. They can be found throughout London where there is plenty of relatively undisturbed cover (dense undergrowth, piles of stones or logs, for example) for somewhere safe to hibernate. They need soft, loose soil in which to burrow underground. The Essex and Middlesex Filter Beds (Waltham Forest) have slow worms, as do Devonshire Road Nature Reserve (Lewisham) and Birdbrook Road Reserve (Greenwich). These are interesting because they are all examples of Slow Worm sites in areas with large human populations. Other Slow Worm colonies probably lie undiscovered in many parks, areas of rough ground and even private gardens.

The only other lizard you are likely to stumble upon in London is the **Common Lizard** (it sometimes goes by the great name, the **Viviparous Lizard**). Big ones will just about fit into an adult's hand with their tails being about half their full length. As with

the other reptiles we have read about, common lizards can come in a variety of different colours - dark green, reddish-brown or even grey on top with a pale underside. When they are caught they will often shed their tails but, unlike the Slow Worm, these will grow back in time.

These lizards emerge from their hibernation quite early in spring and can, if approached quietly, be watched sunning themselves on top of a favourite pile of rocks or logs. Dinner comes in the form of insects, spiders and the usual slugs and snails. And in turn the lizards themselves are a tasty snack for birds, hedgehogs and domestic cats. This somewhat limits their presence in private gardens. But you will find common lizards in many sites in Greater London, such as Wimbledon Common, the Essex and Middlesex Filter Beds in Waltham Forest and alongside the slow worms of the LWT Birdbrook Road Reserve and Honor Oak Adventure Playground Nature Reserve in Lewisham.

In south-east London a small group of **wall lizards** have established themselves (they were released here in the late 1970s) and, as they can be considerably bigger than the Common Lizard, you will probably know if you have seen one!

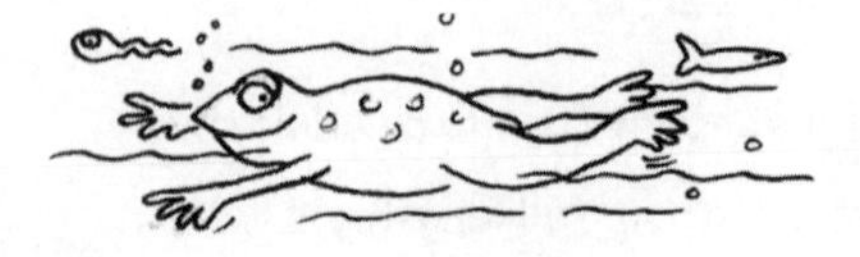

If you have no luck finding lizards or snakes then you shouldn't have too much trouble discovering the **Common Frog**. In fact, there are probably more frogs in London than there are in much of the surrounding countryside, where many of the ponds, which the frogs need to breed in, have been destroyed. So, if you have a garden, the best thing you can do for frogs is to build a garden pond - and then see what other wonderful wildlife comes to visit!

Whatever help you can bring them, frogs still have a lot to contend with in the city, what with cats, birds, rats, hedgehogs, foxes and other predators (that simply means animals which hunt and feed on them) finding them very tasty indeed. Frogs have also been recently exposed to a virus which is killing large numbers of them in some parts of the country.

There is no need to describe the frog to you here as I'm sure you know exactly what they look like and many of you will know just where to find them. If you do want some help, though, try any of the big parks, gardens or some of the smaller reserves such as Park Road Ponds (Hillingdon), Cannon Hill Common (Merton), Plough Lane Pond (Southwark), Kidbrook Green (Greenwich), Grenville Place (Maida Vale) or Camley Street Natural Park in Camden.

We do have another species of Frog in the city but this one is much harder to find. It is the introduced **Marsh Frog** (meaning it isn't native to Britain). It first appeared in the UK near Romney Marshes in 1935. Since then it has spread to a few other locations including Richmond Park, Crane Park Island Nature Reserve and the Wetland Centre at Barnes.

Marsh frogs are very similar to common frogs and it usually takes an expert to tell them apart but they do tend to be more greenish on top than the Common Frog (which is generally more brownish) and they are usually a little bigger. In fact they have been known to eat their smaller common cousins! **Edible frogs** also occur in at least one spot, Walthamstow Marshes, and there is a well established colony not far south of the M25 in Surrey.

Larger and wartier than its froggy relatives is the **Common Toad**. One really good way to tell them apart is that the toad takes small hops and seems to walk, whereas the frog takes bigger leaps. The so-called warts on a toad are actually glands which contain a poisonous substance. This is a very handy device that stops other animals from trying to eat them!

As with frogs, toads hibernate and their diet and habitat are also very similar. However they can be much more aggressive than frogs, and the males are known especially to get into some pretty nasty fights over female toads they fancy.

Toads prefer longer grass than frogs for hunting and bigger ponds in which to lay their spawn. So this gives you a hefty clue as to where you can locate them - and they can gather in huge numbers where they spawn!

It was recorded some years ago that the rare **Natterjack Toad** found a home in South London, but they don't seem to have been seen here for many, many years. But keep your eyes peeled, you just never know.

For a while the huge and escaped **African Clawed Toad** took up residence in a pond in south-east London but it is thought that these have now died out - but who can be sure? Also in South London, small colonies of **yellow bellied toads** persist, having been introduced and spread into garden ponds there.

Newts are not unlike small dragons and for most of the year they can be found in or close to water, so many of the spots mentioned above will also contain a newt community.

There are three types of Newt in Britain today and by far the most common of these is the aptly named **Common** (or **Smooth**) **Newt**. These animals rarely grow longer than an adult's big finger. They have bright orange bellies (which are more brilliant in the males), and their backs are greenish-brown, spotted with black. This beautiful colouring more than makes up for their unspectacular size.

In winter they lie dormant (another word for being in hibernation) under logs, waiting for warmer weather to arrive when they set off for their breeding ponds. Being quite a tasty morsel for fish, newts tend to live in the smaller ponds that do not hold fish and wildlife garden ponds are ideal for this - as they are for frogs.

In addition to those froggy places mentioned earlier (where you are just as likely to spy common newts) you might try Norwood Grove, Devonshire Road Nature Reserve (Lewisham) or the LESSA Pond in Greeenwich.

Palmate Newts are also present in the city but their distribution is more patchy than the Smooth Newt and they tend to turn up more often in the southern parts of Greater

London than anywhere else. They look quite a lot like smooth newts, but are a tiny bit smaller.

By comparison, the **Great Crested** (or **Warty**) **Newt** is a giant – reaching up to 15 centimetres long (that's about the size of an adult's hand). It can often look as if it's almost black, but most are dark brown, with a black-spotted orange belly. The males also have the long, ragged crest down their backs and tails, which give the animal its name. Great crested newts prefer larger and quite weedy waters but unfortunately they are not very common. Britain is considered to be a stronghold for the species (meaning it's one of the best places to find them) but it has been declining at a frightening rate over the past few decades. London's population of great crested newts is quite spread out but, if you're lucky enough to find them, you may well find lots of them. One of the best places in the whole country to go searching for them is in the ponds of Epping Forest.

Their behaviour is like that of their smaller newt cousins but they will attack and eat large insects, including dragonflies almost as long as themselves, and other bigger creatures such as leeches.

For something even more out of the ordinary, parts of south-east London may still hold a few **Alpine Newts**, following their introduction to that part of the country early in the twentieth century.

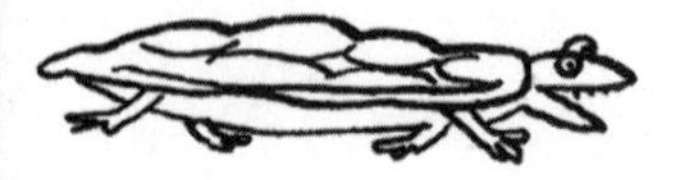 

If you keep your eyes peeled, you might occasionally meet up with some other (and more exotic) introduced or escaped amphibians and reptiles in London. You only need venture to Highgate Ponds to see **American red-eared terrapins**, which have grown as large as dinner plates and are gobbling up as many of the young ducklings and baby moorhens and coots that they can grab in their powerful, beak-like jaws. Terrapins can also be found in various other London ponds including the village pond in Ickenham. I saw a particularly large specimen, some years ago, swimming downstream in a Buckinghamshire brook not far from the capital. These animals are most likely to be discarded pets and our summers are probably not warm enough for them to breed successfully. But with global warming there's no saying what might happen!

A word of warning, though! Don't try and pick them up (even if you can catch them) as they can give a very nasty bite.

Chapter Five

Slime, Scales and Fins

Fish in London

Not long ago, a young man in London went to see his doctor. He had been swimming in the Thames estuary and had emerged with a curious round wound (about the size of a new penny) on his waist. After some investigation it was discovered that the sore had been caused by a **Sea Lamprey**. Have you ever heard of one of those?

Well, first of all I should tell you that what had happened to the man was quite rare and that he was soon well with no ill effects. The wound was caused by the sucker-like disc, ringed with numerous sharp tiny teeth, which the Lamprey has for a mouth.

The reason this was so unusual is that sea lampreys are parasites (this is an animal which lives off another animal or a plant which lives off another plant) and stick to large sea fish. Presumably our unfortunate swimmer must have looked just like one! Mind you, he couldn't have tasted very nice, because the lamprey concerned soon went elsewhere for its dinner. Lampreys are like underwater snakes and can reach up to a metre in length, spending most of their lives out at sea. In spring, however, adults migrate up rivers to spawn. Having performed this vital task they then, sadly, die. Sea lampreys have recently been found as far up the Thames as Barnes but you would be very lucky ever to see one - and more unlucky again to be bitten by one!

Two close relatives of the Sea Lamprey are the **Lampern** and the **Brook Lamprey** which, although smaller in size, are very similar in most other respects. However, there's one big difference with the Brook Lamprey, as you can probably guess by its name. It spends all its time in small rivers and streams. Both of these strange creatures are distributed throughout the Greater London area.

Something which you can see and which, if anything, is more frightening-looking than a Lamprey is an **Eel**. If you go down to Kew Gardens and head for the formal lake near the Palm House and throw some bread in where all the ducks gather to be fed, there is a good chance you will see a huge, slimy head appear from out of the murky, green depths and snap down the crust you have just thrown in.

I have seen some monster eels do this at Kew and I am sure there are plenty of other places in London where these fish have learned to take advantage of people feeding the ducks. It is quite strange behavior for an eel, though, as their normal diet consists of frogs, newts, fish and pond snails.

However, before we give the eel a bad name you may be surprised to learn that it is one of the most remarkable and mysterious creatures in the animal kingdom.

Every single eel that exists in the whole of Europe is born in the Sargasso Sea, which is thousands of miles away, near the Caribbean Islands. The young eels are small and transparent and they spend the next three years travelling up to Europe's rivers. In our case, it's the Thames.

After this stage, they turn into what we call elvers, when they move up into streams and ponds. Here they spend the next several years growing into big adults – turning yellow and then black on their backs and silver on their bellies.

When it's time for them to spawn, they go all the way back down the rivers, sometimes crawling over land to reach them, and make their long return to the Sargasso Sea. Here, after they've spawned, they die. Aren't they incredible?

Almost any pond, river, lake (and even the sewers) in London will be host to eels. They have even become a favourite food for many Londoners, though I believe it's an acquired taste.

If, when you think of fish, you picture the sort of size of your average cod in batter, then think again! Some of the **Pike** that swim around in many of London's waterways can grow as heavy as a six-year-old child - and perhaps even heavier in some of the big London reservoirs. Like the Eel, they mainly eat other fish and frogs, but they will also take young water-birds from the surface. There are stories of them even gulping down small dogs taking a swim!

A look inside the Pike's mouth makes it plain why this fish is known as the **Freshwater Shark** for it has lots and lots of very sharp teeth in its big jaws. However, if you ever go fishing for these predators then please handle them carefully for, despite their fearsome looks, they are quite delicate fish.

The biggest fish you are likely to encounter, however, is the **Carp**. This fish is not native to the United Kingdom but was introduced from the Orient a long, long time ago as they were easy to keep and quite nutritious to eat. Soon, of course, some escaped from the fish-ponds where they were stocked for food and began to spread.

Today, many carp are bred in fish hatcheries and put into London's lakes and ponds (including most of the big parks) for anglers to catch - and then put back, of course! Carp are the 'big brothers' of the **Goldfish**. Goldfish can be found in a number of London ponds, where they have been deliberately introduced. These often come from those fairground prizes, and are slipped straight from the clear plastic bag into the nearest patch of water.

There is, in fact, an even larger fish which has turned up in the Thames in

London (again an 'introduced' species) and this is the Wels Catfish. This enormous animal (the world record was one as heavy as five fully grown men and over 16 feet long!) could probably win first prize in the 'Ugliest Creature of the Year' competition. It has slimy skin and fleshy whisker-like 'fingers' that hang from its mouth, which it uses for its food. However, you are very unlikely to see one of these monsters, unless you are an angler, although they exist in a number of London's waters, including Berwick Ponds (Rainham), where there is a well-known catfish that is about 18 kilograms in weight!

More familiar than all of these are the Roach, Perch, Minnows and Sticklebacks which abound in most London waters. After that, Chub, Bream and Tench are all commonplace.

Even the **Flounder**, a flat estuary-fish like a small plaice, is now found quite far up the Thames. There are much more unusual species making more and more regular appearances as the River Thames and its smaller rivers and streams become cleaner again. Things like Tadpole Fish, Pipefish, Angler Fish and even Sea Horses have even been begun to be recorded.

Perhaps the best news of all is that the Thames is now so clean that **Salmon** are, once again, swimming up the river and may soon breed again in their spawning grounds in the River Kennet after an absence of nearly 200 years – the last Thames salmon of the nineteenth and twentieth centuries was caught in 1833!

Chapter Six

Snappers, Snippers and Pinchers
The Crustaceans of London

This might be the shortest chapter in this short book but it is, I hope, interesting all the same. It is also one of the most disturbing parts of the book because most of it concerns animals which have arrived here by mistake and which now threaten our own native wildlife.

One of these threatened species is the **White-foot Crayfish**, which is like a small, freshwater lobster, complete with a pair of quite powerful-looking pincers. Found in clean ponds, lakes, streams and some reservoirs throughout London, the Crayfish hides away for much of the day, coming out at night to feed on snails, dead fish and even its own smaller brothers and sisters. It, in turn, is eaten by perch, herons, eels, mink and chub. Oh, and by humans in fancy restaurants.

The **European Crayfish** exists in London too but it is the introduced **Signal Crayfish** which is the baddie in all this, for it is this American species which has been taking over from our own Crayfish. In some places the Signal Crayfish numbers have grown so high that they are literally crawling all over the bottom of some canals, rivers and ponds, hoovering up every bit of food that appears. On one stretch of a London canal fishermen can't catch any fish any more because as soon as their bait goes into the water a signal crayfish grabs at it!

Another unwelcome, although so far less numerous, 'invader' is the **Chinese Mitten Crab**. It probably arrived here in the water tanks of ships from the Far East. It was first noted in the Thames in 1932 and has been found here again more recently. Its name comes from the fact that its claws are covered in dense hairs - looking just like furry mittens.

The member of the crustacean family which you are most likely to watch is the **Woodlouse**, of which there are several different species. I'm sure they're familiar to you, but did you know that they have been around for millions of years and can almost be thought of as 'living fossils'? A quick look under large stones or logs will almost guarantee you a good number of these 'armoured' creatures as they scuttle for cover - but do remember to replace the stone or log as you are disturbing the home of any number of tiny bugs and beetles as well.

What Now?

Wherever you go looking for wildlife in London, do so with care for yourself and for the animals that live there too.

Why not get involved and do something to help as well? You could enourage your school to start a wildlife garden or pond in your school grounds. If you have a garden, you could ask your parents to leave a part of it wild and see all the wild visitors who come to it.

Everybody can do something.

On the next few pages you will find some suggestions of what you can do each season to help improve London's wildlife. I'd like to thank the London Wildlife Trust for providing some great ideas. If you want more information and even more ideas then you can go to their website at **www.wildlondon.org.uk** or write to them. You'll find the postal address at the back of the book.

Get your wellies on!

Winter and Spring

Hideyholes for frogs

Build a pile of stones, bricks or logs near your garden pond, if you have one. Not only will frogs hide and hunt there in the summer, but they'll have a nice place to snooze in the winter!

Birdwatch

Different birds like to eat different things in different ways. Some like to eat food hanging from a bird feeder, some like to perch on a bird table and some like to stay with their feet firmly on the ground. Try and identify how different species like to eat. But always remember to put your table in a cat-free place!

If you have a birdbath, or you can put a shallow bowl of water in a cat-free zone, watch how different species of birds bathe - do they put their heads in first or their tails?

Out in the Cold

As we know, not all animals hibernate. Those that do, do so because there is a shortage of food in the winter. And so those left behind need an extra helping hand. Mice and voles are vegetarian, so they would appreciate a wee saucer of sunflower seeds or gerbil food every now and again. Best not to make this a habit, however, as you may start attracting rats.

Squirrel Proof

While we don't want to prevent squirrels from eating, they can be very clever about getting food meant for birds. See if you can design a bird feeder that only birds can use. Prepare to be challenged!

Green Survey

Why not do a survey with your friends or as a class (ask your teacher)? Make a list of the five things that you would change. For example, here's one:

The problem: Litter

Its effect on me: It makes me feel bad

Its effect on the environment: It makes the place look scruffy

The Solution: More litter bins, more recycling, encouraging people to take their litter home with them

You might find your list gets much longer! But you'll see with a little bit of effort how much can be achieved.

Summer

Busy Bees

Get an adult to drill some holes in an old log. Make them different sizes, up to 1cm wide. Solitary bees and wasps may lay their eggs there.

Follow a bee. Does it alwasy choose the same kind of colour or flower?

Dragonfly Danger

At least three of Britain's 42 types of dragonfly are now extinct. This is mainly due to the loss of suitable water sites. Look for ponds on old maps of your area (you'll probably find these at your local library). Are they still there? Older neighbours or relatives might know about changes which have happened to dragonfly homes in your area. Perhaps you could help a dragonfly by building a home for it.

Plant Some Wildflowers

1. Choose packets of seeds which say they're only from *British* wildflowers.

2. Give them a pretend winter by putting them in the fridge for 3 weeks.

3. Get a seed tray ready. Fill it with ordinary garden soil and water it well. Mix the seeds with sand and sprinkle them over the soil. Then trickle more soil over them, just until you can't see them any more.

4. Tie the tray inside a big polythene bag and put it out in the garden until the little seedlings show. A shady place is best.

5. Take the polythene bag off as soon as you can see tiny leaves. But protect the tray from blackbirds by covering the tray with some netting.

6. Plant your wildflowers as soon as they are big enough. Read the seed packet to find which place in the garden is best for each kind.

A Load of Rubbish

Well, not just any kind of rubbish.

Why not make a compost heap - this is a good way of recycling some waste, it's good for the garden and has the added benefit of helping hedgehogs in the winter. Be careful in the winter, however, if you are turning over the compost heap in case you do have some hibernating friends there!

How to make a compost heap:

Materials: A wooden box or chicken wire frame in the shape of a box, built on bare ground. A piece of carpet to cover it once all the ingredients have gone in.

Ingredients: Air and water. Soft cardboard, potato peel, egg boxes, soft garden prunings, rabbit or guinea pig litter. Soft leaves, fruit, vegetables, grass cuttings (in small quantities), nettles.

Method: A month after you've filled up your bin with these ingredients and covered it over with the piece of carpet, turn the pile over with a fork to get some more air into it. If it is dry, water it with the hose. The pile will be ready to use in the garden 6 months/one year later.

Be warned! There are some things you mustn't put in the compost heap: any seeds of weeds or diseased leaves and plants, metal, plastic, droppings from animals that eat meat (cats and dogs), wads of paper or wood, which take too long to rot down.

Autumn

The Pond!

Garden ponds are one of the most important things you can have to attract wildlife. Somebody said a garden is like a motorway service station. Creatures fill up with fuel in the garden just as a car fills up with petrol. Ponds provide habitats for all kinds of wonderful creatures - frogs and toads, newts, water snails, water beetles, dragonflies and damselflies. Remember that when you start to bring wildlife into your garden, other creatures will follow.

We're going to look at how you can become frog-friendly through building a pond.

The best time to build a pond is in the autumn. You will need an adult to help you, but you can start planning the shape and size of it. Your local garden centre will advise you on the best way to line your pond and the best plants for wildlife.

Frogs need ponds for reproduction - but it isn't just water they need. It's important how the pond is built, what plants you put in it, and how you care for your pond.

Make sure your pond has gentle shelving edges rather than a sheer drop - not only will the frogs love this but it will also help any unfortunate creature, which has fallen in by mistake, escape.

Put some plants in round the edges - yellow flag and brooklime are good, along with some tall grasses. Frogs like to hide in them.

There are plants which come under the name 'oxygenators' which you should put in new ponds: they give somewhere for tadpoles to hide, but they will probably need to be cleaned out quite regularly. Two examples are hornwort and starwort.

Remember to clear your pond of weeds in the winter.

And why not keep a diary of frog spawn development? Record when the spawn was spotted, when the back and front legs started to develop, and when the tail disappeared.

Go wild!

Where else can I go?

The best place to start is probably your local borough council. The local library will have details of wildlife sites and projects in your area, and if you have access to the internet, most councils have very good websites including this kind of information. Whatever you do, make sure you follow the 'Country Code' even though you are in the city – in other words, don't drop litter, don't pick flowers and don't disturb the wildlife.

Here are a few organizations and wildlife groups which you can join and which will give you lots more information on where to go to see the best wildlife London has to offer

British Trust for Ornithology (BTO), The Nunnery, Thetford, Norfolk, IP24 2PU. www.bto.org

English Nature, Northminster House, Peterborough, PE1 1UA. www.english-nature.org.uk

Essex Wildlife Trust, Fingringhoe Wick Nature Reserve, Colchester, Essex, CO5 7DN. www.essexwt.org.uk

Hertfordshire and Middlesex Wildlife, Grebe House, St Michaels Street, St Albans, Hertfordshire, AL3 4SN.

Hillingdon Wildlife Trust, 42 Middleton Drive, Pinner, HA5 2PG

Kent Wildlife Trust, Tyland Barn, Sandling, Maidstone, Kent ME14 3BD. www.kentwildlife.org.uk

London Bat Group, c/o Monkleigh Road, Mordern, Surrey SM4 4EQ. www.cix.co.uk/~pguest

London Natural History Society, 18 Zenoia Street, London SE22 8HP. www.users.globalnet.co.uk/~lnhsweb

London Wildlife Trust, Harling House, 47-51 Great Suffolk Street, London SE1 0BS. www.wildlondon.org.uk

London Zoo, Regent's Park, London NW1 4RY. www.weboflife.co.uk

National Trust, 36 Queen Anne's Gate, London SW1H 9AS. www.nationaltrust.org.uk

Natural History Museum, Cromwell Road, London SW7 5BD. www.nhm.ac.uk

Royal Society for the Protection of Birds Reserve (RSPB), The Lodge, Sandy, Bedfordshire, SG19 2DL. www.rspb.org.uk

The Wetland Centre, Queen Elizabeth's Walk, Barnes, London SW13 9WT (this is part of the WWT, below). www.wetland-centre.org.uk

The Wildfowl and Wetland Trust (WWT), Slimbridge, Gloucestershire, GL2 7BT. www.wwt.org.uk

The Wildlife Trusts, The Kiln, Waterside, Mather Road, Newark, Nottinghamshire, NG24 1WT (this is the part of the same organization as The London Wildlife Trust and will direct you to sites further afield from London). www.wildlifetrusts.org

The Woodland Trust, Autumn Park, Grantham, Lincolnshire, NG31 6LL. www.woodland-trust.org.uk

If you enjoyed this book, why not try others in the series:

CRYPTS, CAVES AND TUNNELS OF LONDON
by Ian Marchant
Peel away the layers under your feet and discover
the unseen treasures of London beneath the streets.
ISBN 1-904153-04-6

GRAVE-ROBBERS, CUT-THROATS AND POISONERS OF LONDON
by Helen Smith
Dive into London's criminal past and meet some of its
thieves, murderers and villains.
ISBN 1-904153-00-3

DUNGEONS, GALLOWS AND SEVERED HEADS OF LONDON
by Travis Elborough
For spine-chilling tortures and blood-curdling punishments,
not to mention the most revolting dungeons and prisons you
can imagine.
ISBN 1-904153-03-8

THE BLACK DEATH AND OTHER PLAGUES OF LONDON
by Natasha Narayan
Read about some of the most vile and rampant diseases ever
known
and how Londoners overcame them – or not!
ISBN 1-904153-01-1

GHOSTS, GHOULS AND PHANTOMS OF LONDON
by Travis Elborough
Meet some of the victims of London's bloodthirsty monarchs,
murderers, plagues, fires and famines - who've chosen to stick
around!
ISBN 1-904153-02-X

In case you have difficulty finding any Watling St books in your local bookshop, you can place orders directly through

BOOKPOST
Freepost
PO Box 29
Douglas
Isle of Man
IM99 1BQ

Telephone: 01624 836000
e-mail: bookshop@enterprise.net